KATRINA

KATRINA

BY LYN LIFSHIN

POETIC MATRIX PRESS

Front Cover Photo Credit: NASA/Jeff Schmaltz, MODIS Land
Rapid Response Team Updated August 29, 2005 8:20 a.m. EDT.

Poor Richard font is based on the Keystone Type Foundry design,
circa 1919.

ISBN: 978-0-9827343-0-8

Poetic Matrix Press
PO Box 1223
Madera, CA 93639
www.poeticmatrix.com

DEDICATION

TO THE PEOPLE CAUGHT UP IN KATRINA

PREFACE

We have all been touched by the major disasters that have filled the internet and cable news channels over the past few years including the earthquakes in Chile and Haiti; the Indian Ocean earthquake that spond the massive tsunami, and the devastation of Katrina that left New Orleans in such a state. Katrina touched the closest to home but in this world we are brought close up to peoples all over and we cannot deny them.

The Great Tangshan Earthquake in China in 1976 killed over 250,000 Chinese but at the time it was little more than a few lines in the newspaper and seconds on the evening news. The reporting at the time could not gather up the horror of that event as we can today.

Still what we have mostly missed in all the reporting is the intimacy of a poet's voice who can bring the real right up inside us. Lyn Lifshin's volume of straight forward, exact poetry in KATRINA does this. There is a clear ungarnished force to her words that gives us the chance to bring our own sense of loss, grief and compassion into the lives of those who have been drawn into such an event. Through Lyn's words we know better how to understand our own feelings and through them the feelings of our fellow humans in their moments of tragedy. Maybe we will, as well, gain a better understand of those in our own communities.

The Super Bowl of 2010 was what I call a minor drama. For those involved it is important indeed, and yet, in the grand scheme it passes mostly unnoticed once the game has ended. This time, because of the teams involved, the New Orleans Saints and the Indianapolis Colts, the game played out in the symbolic realm as well. With the Saints' win many across the country could better join with the still suffering people of New Orleans and the gulf coast; could join again in their loss, grief and rise with compassion to celebrate with them in this minor drama that even for a moment in passing could eclipse the major drama of KATRINA.

Can poetry be a place, as well, to rise up in compassion? Lyn's voice does this. She speaks of individual dramas, not minor but unique, in the lives of those who experienced the major drama of KATRINA. She adds to the great heart that connects us to each other from New Orleans to Chile to Haiti to Indonesia to China in 1976, and to all who live through major dramas, minor dramas, and the tragic moments of our individual lives; to those who live in sadness and, oh yes, in joy as well.

John Peterson, publisher

Contents

KATRINA

I

ROSALIE GUIDRY DOSTE, 100

survived 5 days on a
suffocating 2nd floor
flooded New Orleans
nursing home only
to die soon after she
was rescued

ODESSA HURLEY WAS A FAMILIAR FIGURE

walking along the streets
of Biloxi during the
day light hours, passing
out religious tracts and
gathering treasures in
the bag she carried. *She
had sneakers on a mile
too big for her and big
white sox pulled up
to her knees* said Cleo
Meaut, 74, a long time
church friend. *She wasn't
what you called poor
but she looked poor, gave
all her money to charity.
She would send money off
to missionaries to help
them out and when I
say money, I mean a
good bit of money.*
According those the town
people, she lived all her
life in Biloxi, decades in
the same small house with
out a TV or other creature
comforts. She outlived two
husbands. Her life revolved
around her daily walks
all over Biloxi. One woman
said *she told me on Saturday
night at church, I hope God
gives me 10 more years*

because I'm not finished
with my work here on earth.
I'm trying to buy my way into
heaven. Father was standing
there and he said oh Miss
Odessa, you know you can't
buy your way to heaven
and she just laughed. Miss
Odessa refused to leave her
home. She had survived plenty
of storms. Her friend says
when she heard she drowned
she said many prayers for her
friend but said Miss Odessa
probably did okay on her own.

As One Man Sat in an Evacuation Center in Baton Rouge

he could not stop watching
the images of hurt and
crying children on TV.
Known as Grandpa Grady
the elderly man in his
River Ridge neighborhood
was sickened by the images,
was saying "ya'll get those
children." To calm him,
family members lied
and reassured him they
would rescue the children
he was seeing on TV.
But as the day wore on,
sounds grew quieter
and he stopped eating or
speaking. A nurse stopped
by but did not send him
to a hospital. Last Thursday
he died in a single bed
in a small room at the shelter.
"I think," his daughter
said, he grieved him
self to death"

ONE TWIN, IN CHICAGO, WALKING HORSES

wishes she had been more alert
during her sister's last phone
call, that she'd made her
sister know she could
survive a flood in the
middle of darkness. My
sister, she says, was
brilliant, the most creative
thing I've known, she had
challenges. And I was the
one who was able to function
a little better. All my life
I've saved my sister and I'm
just tormented I didn't
save her and I could have.
We shared a house, a shot
gun house each of us with
one side of the dwelling.
My cats, Petrouchka
and Svetlana running
back and forth. My sister,
a recovering alcoholic
was not working but had
many deep interests—
ballet, figure skating
and old movies. She was
a vehement critic of the
establishment when they
did her wrong. I'll always
think of her in long color-
ful sundresses and
vintage shawls. Now, I

wish I'd cleared access to
the attic or bought a small
boat, assembled some
kind of kit for emergencies.
All she needed was a
reason to be

86 YEAR OLD PEARLINE CHAMBERS

spent two days alone in her
one story house in the
submerged 9th ward,
flood water to her neck.
She lost her false teeth,
her new wig and her cats.
"I just wandered around
and wandered around,
trying to get up in my
attic," the widow said.
"I kept climbing and
slipping and falling in
that water." After she was
rescued, two men floating
by on a board heard her
screams. She spent two
more semi conscious
days in the city trying
to walk, severely de-
hydrated and hungry.
"I didn't know where I
was. I laid somewhere,
I'm not sure where. People
walked around me." Two
weeks after the storm,
Chambers feels fine
living now with her
sister's family in this
small town in Louisiana.
She said she "has no
body but my stubborn

self to blame for ignoring
hurricane warnings,
refusing to flee in her
blue Chevrolet Corsica"

Katrina Evacuees in Texas School Fight

a fight between a group
of displaced New Orleans
students and their class
mates ended with three
teenagers hospitalized
and five under arrest.
The morning fight at
Jones High School
started after a student
from Houston threw a
soft drink can into a
group of New Orleans
students. One student
from New Orleans was
treated for facial cuts
and two Houston teens
for face and rib injuries.
20 to 25 students got
involved. The quickest
way to earn a ticket out
of Jones High School and
into detention is to hurt
one of these students

IT'S DARK, IT'S SHIRT-SOAKING HOT

and the only word to
describe the heavy
odor is "indescribable."
Still, they refuse to leave.
Even the sight of corpses
tied to banisters to stop
them from drifting failed
to drive off straggling
New Orleans homeless.
Some finally say "I've
had enough." They're
running out of food.
There are human remains
in different houses. *The*
smell messes with your
psyche. One woman stays
so she can take care of
her parents who are
disabled. She walks
around waving a white
flag so no one mistakes
her for a looter

St Bernard Parish and Plaque Mines was Ground Zero

In Charlevelle, cars
were swallowed, the
homes shattered
and people left
clinging for life.
Survivors waited
more than a week
since Katrina cut its
swath along the
Gulf Coast. Word
is only now starting
to trickle out. *If you
dropped a bomb on
this place it could
not be any worse.*
Homes were chopped
open. A Baptist Church
roof ripped off. 30
residents in a nursing
home died. 1 to 20
feet of water. Water
gurgling in spurts.
Natural gas leaks. *I
can't even imagine
trying to rebuild*

I Can't Even Imagine Trying to Rebuild This

a wildlife officer
said, looking for
survivors. As
relief efforts
sputtered, an
out of work
electrician took
charge. He trans
formed his parents'
bar and seafood
restaurant into
a shelter where
he sent people to
clear roads, hook
up generators.
About 20 people
have been staying
there these days,
On a boarded up
window out front
is a blue spray
painted sign:
ABOUT TIME BUSH

BILOXI

trees across the highway

large boats in people's
front yards

close to the beach
the destruction is worse

40 or 50 cars on
top of each other

stacked three high.
The town ink black, a

line of clouds
going east to west

onyx night sky
with thousands of stars

II

130 TO 150 BODIES A DAY

in the temporary mortuary

fingerprints, x rays, DNA.
After that officials
will turn the bodies
over to Louisiana officials
and then to the families

some bodies so decomposed
DNA will be the
only identification

It Was as if All of Us Were Already Pronounced Dead

behind a cardboard sign:
SHELTER FROM HELL.
Trash barrels overflow.
For 5 days, 20,000 waited
to be rescued, not just from
the flood water but from
the nightmarish place
they sough refuge. The
moon that hovered over
the center seemed closer
than help. Rapes and
murders, robberies,
fathers trying to protect
their family. "It was as if
somebody already had
the body bags. Wasn't no
body coming to get us."
No one knows how many
died, were raped, assaulted.
250 National Guards
camped out but did nothing.
Everywhere I went one
woman said, I saw people
with guns in their hands
putting guns to other
people's heads

It was as if All of Us Were Already Dead

Recounting her please for
milk for her babies, for
food, for protection, one
woman described the
sense of bewilderment
and anger. "Surreal."
she said on live TV.
"This is America," one
other woman shouted
into a TV. What she meant
was *this is not supposed
to happen here*

ONE MAN GOT HIS DAUGHTERS OUT OF THEIR HOME

put them in a crate,
tied the crate with rope
to his waist then began
swimming. He hustled
his way, finally, onto a
motor boat. It sped off
to the Superdome, all
aboard, exhausted. At
the dome, they were
rebuffed, pointed to
the Convention Center
10 blocks away. By the
time he got there, with
the crate and his two
daughters, he found him
self gazing into thousands
of bewildered faces.
Gripping his daughters,
he walked fast, exactly
where, he didn't know
but he passed an elderly
lady who was listing in
a wheel chair. *I went
down the hall* he said.
*By the time I was back,
she was already gone.*
He spent 4 days at the
center. All he had for him
self and the two girls
was a sandwich and two
bottles of water from
a stranger

one woman arrived with
2 children, 6 and 2. "Soon
as I got there I saw fighting.
I saw people throwing
chairs, pull a gun out right
in front of little children."
She saw a boy who could
not breathe, asthma or panic.
She pointed it out to one
police man she saw and the
officer checked the boy,
said there was nothing they
could do. The boy was dead.
Another officer appeared.
The others figured he would
remove the body but the
officer said it was just to
check some gun shots

CONVENTION CENTER NIGHTMARE II

a gang broke into the
locked alcohol storage
area and suddenly had
200 cases of hard liquor
and 200 cases of beer.
Before long, there were
scenes of gangsters,
drunk, groping young
girls and not far, women
in corners, balled up,
frozen

SUPER DOME NIGHTMARE

in the blackness, every
one was afraid. Street
savvy teens who thought
they could handle the
streets suddenly were
shaking. Even police
officers were scared,
took off their uniforms
and threw their badges
down

SUPERDOME

one man saw prostate bodies
near the bathroom, dead
or unconscious, he didn't
know. He was carrying his
two daughters, 1 and 4, told
them it was ok to soil themselves

rumors were treated
as fact, at one time
rumors of 200 bodies
brought coroners
rushing in. One night
one deranged man
started yelling "Here
comes the water." A
panic started. Mothers
grabbed children. The
deaf didn't know what
was happening. The
old couldn't move. A
woman screamed some
one was stepping on
her baby. At one point,
a police car drove up:
perhaps good news. He
threw out a few bottles
of water igniting a free
for all. One man struck
another with a 2 by 4.
That man was split in
the heat. "He was leaking"
someone says, "He just
dropped, face first"

SUPERDOME NIGHTMARE

2 women were arguing,
one plunged a pair of
scissors into the shoulder
of the woman she'd been
fighting with. Others
broke into the kitchen to
try to cook something
and a fire broke out.
Some colleagues locked
themselves in an office.
A gang rattled the door,
threatened to break
down the door

MIRACLE

the man, the father
who swam his two
daughters to safety
before they all
arrived at the
convention center,
headed out as he
had arrived, his two
little girls, his
everything in the
crook of his arms

AFTER THE CENTER EMPTIED OUT

3 days after evacuation
they slipped past the
caution sign to bag
the bodies still inside.
Sitting slumped inside
in a black wheelchair,
a woman about 60 in
a hospital gown, a
man in a shirt and
jogging pants lay
curled up on the
concrete floor, his
hand over his face.
Down the hallway,
a large man, 6'4"
and over 300 lbs
lay with his arms
over his head and his
legs bent. Another
woman in hospital
scrubs lay a few feet
from him next to
aluminum cans and
trays with stained but
elegant white dinner
menus. Around the
bodies were pools
of dried blood.
Looking closer,
abrasions on the
corpses. On the

grey soiled floor,
a pair of shiny brass
knuckles. The dead
had been murdered

ONE MAN REMEMBERS HIS BROTHER'S LAST WORDS

before he leaped into
Katrina's raging water:
"If I don't make it,
make sure my kids do."
The two brothers and
one's girlfriend tied
3 children with straps
and stepped outside.
A neighbor let them in
so the group hung to
the side of the house.
His brother was the first
to go. When the other
turned his back to the
children, he found his
niece had drowned.
Houses were folding
like paper. Finally he
and the last child
climbed to the roof. He
waited for days. Then
he was airlifted to the
airport. When he got
on the plane, no one told
him where they were:
Chicago. But there, the
group ran into some
red tape and then they
had to go to Michigan.
At the bus, the people
were holding signs

saying "Welcome,"
"We Love You." The
Lord, this last brother
said, "was telling me
it was time for a change."

III

THE ANIMALS, LOST, ABANDONED

the dogs are listless,
lethargic or scared.
Terrified, if quivering
means anything. Some
are noisy, the bodacious
brown pit bull looking
on who fixes his eyes
on a visitor and snarls
so intensely one can
imagine him warning
"get me out of here...
or else." One woman is
looking for her dogs,
crying. When the police
rescued her and her 13
year old grandson they
made her leave their
beloved dogs behind,
Scout the Sheltie,
Datsun, the spaniel
and the oldest of then,
a Boston Terrier, Pepe
who had surgery 3
months ago and has
seizures. "They're all
such sweethearts. We
dress them up for
Halloween. Then on
Christmas each wears
a Santa hat. These
dogs are like our
children."

so many stayed, wouldn't
leave their animals. As
rescue boats go thru the
river streets to find humans,
pet rescue boats search for
marooned pets. Sometimes
animals and their owners
are found together. Some
times the animals are
found alone and sick from
drinking the ruined street
water. Some pets are cut,
injured, have infections,
canine dysentery, are so
dehydrated. Instead of
Noah, there are 450
workers here: vets and
staffers from the hundreds
of people everyday who
arrive with hope of good
news. They register,
write down descriptions
of their pets, whether they
are wearing a collar. Many
bring a photograph then
they begin their search
up and down the lanes of
small kennels. They share
stories, share horror stories
like one rumor that police
in a nearby parish shot

dogs on the street. Some
one tells about one dog who
had wanted to be found
so badly, to gain entry
to a house with a barking
dog, rescuers pulled out
the air conditioning unit
and a dog came flying out,
jumped into the arms
of the rescuer

SOME LEFT HUGE BAGS OF DOG FOOD

ripped open
before they left.
Someone left a
pot bellied pig.
Rescuers found it
in its own bed
room with pig
murals on the wall
and family photos
with the pig. Some
one says people
become so attached
to their animals
they have their own
personalities.
One man, a
Jaguar mechanic,
says his dogs know
all the kids names.
The dogs are so close
they have to be
transported in the
same carrier or
a ruckus will
break out. "They
are," a man says,
"like brothers."

WHEN IT WAS LOOKING HOPELESS, WHEN THEY COULDN'T FIND ANY OF THEIR DOGS

forlorn, walking from cage to
cage, no sign of the dogs.
It's depressing and she's
already depressed. She's
been to counseling for
horrors she witnessed on
the streets during the flood.
She says her grandson
probably needs help too.
The day Katrina struck,
she gathered the boy with
the dogs at the hotel she
manages. But flooding forced
her out after 3 days. They
ended up on a street corner.
"Rats were running around.
A very ill man died right
in front of them, a man
whose name they didn't
know but who had a
dog named Rudy, a
dachshund like their Datsun.
When the man died, she
decided to take care of his
dog too. But they had to
leave Rudy behind with
their own dogs. Suddenly, as
his grandmother was speaking
her grandchild came racing
with all his might, all red
in the face, shouting Grandma,
I have found Pepe. They ran to

the end of the row to a small
kennel in a medical ward.
Now the grandmother was
crying flat out. She kissed Pepe
thru the cage letting him lick
her face. "He's the old man,
he's been with us a long time."
"He's going to need to go right
to a veterinary hospital. He
has some serious injuries," a
technician says, "there are deep
lacerations around the little
terrier's neck." Later the vet
said that a large dog bit Pepe,
apparently swung him around
from side to side making
deep toothy gashes and one
of his eyes were scratched
which could lead to blindness."
But Pepe will live and tomorrow
they will come back and look
for the other dogs. "They're
not just animals, "they're my
babies," she says carrying Pepe
toward the parking lot in a white
towel like swaddling clothes

HEARING ROBERT WISE DIED

almost this time of year,
the aspens crackling

the drive out from Boulder
up into the hills

Octoberly crisp.
Peanut soup in an

out of season restaurant.
The Rockies blue.

We were all at the
Denver Film Festival,

would never meet again
but that warm perfect after

noon, none of us could
have believed that

OCTOBERLY

leaves inside out,
drying and the bedroom
staying black the time
of year I think of fall
on Jackson, taking
the bus to class, cloud-
less sky, a red smell
of burning. I was 23,
24 and I thought what
ever mattered was behind
me. Each week, each
Tuesday I began non
stop work on a paper
for the handsome dandy,
the Harvard professor.
Each weekend my new
husband and I drove
to Café Lena and I
imagined a poet or folk
singer might look my
way. Janis Joplin played
at a bar a two minute
walk from our flat.
No admission, no
minimum. I rode on
Josh White's lap
over a bumpy road
upstate. He told my ex
when he coughed, "that
sounds like my come

cough," as he slid his
fingers over my thigh
where no one could see

IN THE SHELL OF A CITY

a summer white dress
hangs in a second story
room framed by green
shutters on an open
window as if someone
had planned to wear it,
as if someone soon will
return to restart a new
life suspended. Or,
maybe not

THE RECEDING FLOOD WATERS ALONG THE STREETS IN MID CITY

revealed two bodies
face down, arms out
stretched, at rest
on a park like media
where the grass
drowned and then
turned straw in
the harsh sun

ACROSS TOWN

mother nature's macabre
handiwork, four small
rusted houses list against
one another, accordion-
style, propelled off their
foundations by the
surge of flood waters
from a levee breach
nearby. Dried mud coats
everything, like nuclear
fall out

BOATS AND CARS SMASHED THUR COLLASPED HOMES

Roofs lie about.
Boats and cars smashed
thru collapsed homes.
Roofs attached to
nothing or broken
to bits. Putrid
muck triggers
gags

TWO FRAIL

elderly women
who needed
medical attention
would not leave
till their dog
got attention.
On a stretcher
one said "I
don't go till
Bomba comes,
she's our
family."

IV

DOWN IN THE FONTAINEBLEAU AREA

the watermarks 6 feet high,
visible on some houses.
Signs of life slowly are
returning with the trickle
of residents who've gotten
in to look at what is left.
It's freaky, everything
just floated. I'm going to
spray it all someone says,
spray it down with Clorox.
"Look at my counter
tops. They were so pretty."
"Water knocked my new
refrigerator over, my lovely
mahogany door. I spent
$13,000 this year on my back
yard. It was beautiful. Now
it's a disaster but it's a
fixable disaster."

ON DUMAINE STREET IN THE FRENCH QUARTER

Thomas Wolfe, owner
of the famed Wolfe's of
New Orleans takes a
break from cleaning up
another of his three
restaurants. He lost his
stock of pancetta and
provolone, his art is
in cheeses, not to mention
the deserts created by
his pastry chef and the
meringue that exploded
in the searing heat. "The
new New Orleans, I
think it will be a boom
town. I'm hoping it will
be a boom town," he says,
sweat dripping down
his face in his kitchen
turned sauna. "it's
just the spirit, just the
heart that we have
in New Orleans"

QUARTER RATS

what some French Quarter
residents call themselves,
spend nights brainstorming,
dreaming about a new New
Orleans. "What else do we
have to do at night in the
dark but come up with ideas,"
a hotel waiter says. "We've
lived on tuna, chicken,
beans, donated MRE's and
listened to news on battery
powered radios. We'll just
sit and wait and see what
happens"

INSTEAD OF GUMBO AND FRIED OYSTERS AND CRAWFORD BISQUE

and blackened fish, you
have to hold your breath
if you walk past the Acme
Oyster and Seafood Café
on Iberville St in the French
Quarter. An overloaded
dumpster reeks. Bourbon
Street is deserted except
for police cars, military
convoys and two New
York cops walking an
unfamiliar beat. "It's
my first time in New
Orleans. I wish I could
have come before this."
Streets quiet and empty as
the graveyard. Smashed
doors. Thru the second
floor, tables set, white
crisp linen ready for
service. "My Aunt Ella
and my Mom informed me
that we are going to
rebuild and because they
are matriarchs, they're
strong women, we will
rebuild it. We're not
offered a choice on this"

ANTOINES. THE RESTAURANT

on St Louis that
claims it invented
Rockefeller oysters
would not use
ordinary plywood to
cover up the elegant
French doors that
line the first floor.
The plywood was
painted purple, yellow
and green, Mardi
Gras colors

It Won't Be High Cuisine but It Will Be New Orleans

the chef at Restaurant
August known more
for its avant garde
cuisine. These days
he is thinking of big
pots of jambalaya
and old New Orleans
staples. Down the
street, Center Grocery—
looters got into the
store but were quickly
chased away. The
windows and doors
were boarded up. On
each piece of wood
a hand lettered sign:
"Looters will be shot
on sight," signed
Martino Gambino.
"Completely made up,"
the owner said, "we
wanted something
that would scare them"

THE SUN ROSE HIGHER
AND TURNED YELLOW

and no lines formed.
Inside the road block

a weather beaten sign
said "Think Positive,

St Bernard." Dead
horse by the road,

cows grazing. Dogs
roam. A TV dangles

5 feet above a shot
gun house suspended

by a plug attached to the
other side of the wall.

A truck upended in
the water with a bumper

sticker about drugs.

RETURN TO NEIGHBORHOODS THAT AREN'T

East of Violet River in the
area no one is allowed to enter,
a green truck towing a small
metal trailer. 3 riders emerge,
the youngest, a Confederate
flag tattooed on his arm
dressed in camouflage
waders and a t shirt with
a picture of a fish, the men
set out from a kind stranger's
home in Auburndale Florida
and drove thru the night
to get here. There was no
where to sleep in New Orleans.
"Anyway," one of the men
with him said, "I got a lot of
bills, a lot of work." "Dump
Her" on his t shirt. The men
were gathering possessions for
friends and family members
across the county. "Watch
out for snakes," one said
entering one house to look for
rings. Dogs lumbered in the
front yard, panting, staring, then
turned and ran off. The men
waded into the house, into the
living room, then the bed
room. One pushed a mattress
aside and raised an upended
dresser then opened a drawer.
"There it is, this is what I

came for, a couple of rings."
Then the men walked
back over the wooden pilings
and downed branches in the
yard and got into the truck
and drove toward Violet.

GOING BACK

they drove past the Dollar Mart
and the bakery that sold King
Cakes then stopped at one
man's house to get his electric
saw but the mud in his house
was so thick they abandoned
the saw and drove on, past a
Mitsubishi Eclipse on the roof
of a house with white columns.
They drove to Florida Ave,
took pictures of a toilet sitting
there on the foundation, the
rest of the house gone. They
found a piggy bank that said
"college fund" and a couple of
family pictures, walked past
one's daughter's baby doll and
a bottle of home made maple
syrup and got back in the truck.
At another house, they retrieved
photo albums, a National Champ
trophy from a New Orleans
team, a filthy teddy bear and
the wedding dress one's wife
wore. The man collected these
things and then thought better
of it—threw the bear and
the trophy back in the mud.
They drove thru dark oily mud,
past volcanic landscapes of
caked brittle soil, past sand
dumped from trucks, past

refinery fires, a metal barricade
to a place where the mud stood
3 feet in the street. "There
ain't no way to go farther."

the wind and suddenly
the flat glare of July and
August, season of sweat
and sensuality's over.
When you walk out
barefoot for the paper,
bricks are cool. The
maple tree's going
sienna and yellow.
No light in the bed
room until late, the
slant so different. In
just a month, the heat
that slapped you around
retreats. It's getting
dark too early. Shadows
that weren't there a
day ago are. Lights
across the street
go on earlier. More
leaves gone each
morning and heat that
held you like a too
anxious lover, playboy
who wouldn't stay,
a mistress leaving
you cold, edges out,
is leaving you.

THEY DIDN'T ASK YOUR NAME
OR SAY KISS MY BEHIND

he says as he sits at the
table in his backyard.
He's talking about state
troopers who couldn't
give him the time of day.
He has returned to a
place laid low by Katrina.
Trees are jammed thru
the roof, power wires
swoop from tree to tree
like thin black bunting.
He's not leaving, no
matter what anybody tells
them to do. "They'll have
to pull me out with a tow
rope." When he heard
orders to leave, he packed
up his 2003 Cadillac
De Ville and he and his
wife and sister and two dogs
headed north looking for
lodging. "If they want people
to evacuate, you've got to
have a place to evacuate to."
Hours later, around Jackson,
they realized they weren't
going to find a room so
headed back south. They
stopped at a little hunting
camp in Hazelhurst MS
but there was no power.

They did find a 5 gallon
can of gas. "If it weren't
for that we would have been
stuck on the side of the
road." They drove home but
when they got to a security
check, the state trooper said
they had to sleep elsewhere.
"Where?" he asked. A trooper
suggested the Red Cross
Shelter. So they turned around
and motored back north.
They reached the town of
Baton Rouge about 8 pm.
We never heard of where
shelters were. I don't think
they have them.

An Oasis of Gas

lights up the night
in this postage stamp
size city across the
Mississippi from
New Orleans, a
beacon of light
illuminating the
pitch black night.
Ahmid Mashan, a
native who came
here 4 years ago was
out in the parking
lot of his gas station
and power came on so
he says I decided
to open. We had
generators at first and
we were giving gas to
police and town
vehicles and then I
decided to sell to the
people in the neighbor
hood. And the price
was lower than it is
in Washington and
most of the country,
2.99 a gallon, that
was the price it was
before we closed said
Mashan and I thought it
would not be fair to raise

it now. "Why," some
one asked in a sea of
darkness, "was he blessed
with electricity?" "Because
this is the city of West
We Go," he said with a
laugh as though it
needed no further
explanation

UPROOTED, SCATTERED FROM THE FAMILIAR

carrying the scraps of their
lives in plastic trash bags,
citizens of the drowned
city landed in a strange
new place, wondered
where they were. The
land was strange and
nearly everyone they
saw was white. "I'm
not sure where I am,
what do they call this,
the upper west or some
thing," one man said, "we
are getting a lot of love
but we're also getting a
lot of stares like we
were aliens or something."
"Am I the only person
out here, a 30 year old
man says, "with dread locks?"

SEPTEMBER 3

under black water,
mystery and mystery.
A topsy turvey world.
One man knows his
front wall is 11 feet under,
checked the depth finder
on his fishing boat as he
pulled away. In front
of the Super Dome
thousands of tattered,
exhausted people wait
for buses that never seem
to come. Where waters
were chest deep and
rising, a man leaves every
thing but his kids. At
the air port, someone
says on the radio
"Larry is handling
the body issue"

PEOPLE TRUDGED THRU THE CITY

in thousands, some
pushing shopping carts,
some pulling suitcases.
Many carry a few items
in a plastic sack. One
woman tied a rope to
a grey storage container
fashioning a sled that
held her sleeping baby

BENEATH A MISSISSIPPI BRIDGE

a teen age girl sprawled
in a shopping cart, a
white towel around her
ankle. She had been shot
two weeks earlier.
Doctors got the bullet out
but she was in no shape to
walk. On each stretch
of street, someone needed
medicine, oxygen, a
wheel chair, a ride. Every
one needed a ride

You Should Sleep in the Day

and try to stay awake
at night because it's
not as hot another said
and there's another
good reason to stay
awake at night: to
watch for marauders

A FEW STREETS AWAY

Shawn Fitzgerald tried to
comfort her two toddlers
as they waited in blistery
morning sun. She knew
about evacuations before
Katrina hit. Where would
she go? How would she get
there? There was no way.
"I just spent all my money
Friday settling in my condo.
Now the wires are targets

people on the streets.
There's no place
to turn. No leader
ship. What do
you see one woman
asked, "Black
all these black
people, nobody
but us"

"ME AND MY WIFE, WE WERE LIVING

paycheck to paycheck, like
most everybody else in New
Orleans. He was standing
on wobbly thin legs in the
bowels of the semi darkened
Louis Armstrong auditorium
after he had been plucked
by rescuers from a road way.
I don't own a car. Me and my
wife, we travel by public
transportation. The most
money I ever have on me is
$400 and that goes to pay the
rent." He was saddened
knowing he and his wife
could never afford the airfare
to escape. "If I took my
wife out to dinner it was once
a month, to Piccadilly's,
never any movies." A basic
existence

A 47 Year Old Grandmother was Rocking a Grand Child

*these people look at us and
wonder why we stayed behind,
she says. Well, would they
leave their grandparents,
children behind? Look
around, say see you later?*
She gave a roll of her eyes
behind the raised voice. *We
had one vehicle, a truck.
I wanted my family to be
together. They couldn't all
fit in the truck. We had to
decide on leaving family
members or stay.* She shifted
the baby in her arms. *I'm
living pay check to pay check.
My mother died this year.
My real job was a private
duty care taker. I had one
patient. He died two weeks
after my mother died. We've
made around 2500 but that
included help from my son
and husband. They're
missing now*

V

WHY SOME DIDN'T GET OUT

I got $3.00 on me now
a 39 year old man said.
I never had a savings
account. I make $340
a month and stay with
my mother. I give her
150 of that. My income
is for disability. My
hands got burned
bad in a 1993 fire. I
lost my nephew but
saved two kids

ABOUT 2 AM FRIDAY A JANGLING PHONE WOKE ONE MAN FROM A RESTLESS SLEEP

Hearing her voice was
like Christmas. Her
mother remembers
her calling and the first
request of the daughter
who'd left everything
but her laptop, Ipod
and cell phone at Xavier"
Mom, can you take
me shopping. "Can't you
get home first," her
mother thinks? Now
she's back, with her
hair a massive twist and
her body a walking
festival of silver rings
and ear baubles. Was she
nervous? *I don't really*
get nervous she laughs
tho one girl's hair was
falling out and another
was throwing up. It
wasn't the storm she
says, I slept thru that
but it was the heat and
the non flushing toilets
and the mounting un-
certainty. For a long time
it seemed no one knew
we were there

REPLACE

as if you could,
the cafes underwater,
their curtains floating
like a drowning
woman's seaweed
hair. Lost as those
underwater menus,
the ink not ink, the
space as unlike what
it once was full of
the way, like some
one watching light
dissolve or those
with paper streamers
tied to the ones they
left on shore
seeing the ribbons
shimmer on
the water then
disappear

AIN'T NOBODY GOT MONEY

a man who has worked
the same fish boat 22
years sighed. "Right
now I'm out of a job."
It's a scary thing. If
they put us out here
where do we turn?"
The digs are not fancy.
Everyone sleeps on a
church pew. The showers
for men are next door at
the ministers house.
Women are shuttled
down the street. Dinner
arrives on a foam plate
from a church around
the corner, the first
breakfast was consisted
of cold sandwiches Pop
Eye's hadn't yet opened.
I "lot of us are giving out
of our houses" one volunteer
said, "You can't get in
contact with FEMA."

THIS IS ALL I GOT

one man said, stretching
his arms and pointing to
a red t shirt, blue jeans
and a pair of slippers.
"we lost everything."
But that's not his
biggest worry. He has
not seen his wife, kids
or grandchildren since
last Saturday. He heard
they were in Baton Rouge.
One woman was nearly
hysterical Saturday
morning when friends
went to wash clothes.
"I want to go home,"
she yelped, "I can't stay
here forever." Volunteers
have few words of
comfort. "Reality really
hasn't begun to sink
in for these people. They
are still in a state
of shock."

PEOPLE ARE SLEEPING IN THE STREET

someone calls a friend,
says the authorities
said the small shelter
had no kitchen, had
to be shut down.
"Are they losing
their minds?" some
body asks, "those
people were living
outside with no place
to sleep. What could
be more unsanitary
than waking in water
that has feces and
snakes in it."

AT AN AIRPORT TURNED FIELD HOSPITAL

Inside a tent, they were trying
to find a good vein in a
woman with sickle cell
anemia. Next to her, a 12
year old with a rare blood
disease. Down the hall,
the row of green Army
stretchers, a man sucking
on anesthesia in water. The
woman with sickle cell
anemia was freezing.
"We don't have blankets,
Darlin. We just have paper
gowns," the nurse said.

The light oddly beautiful
from inside the white medic
tent, filtered and soft, a surreal
MASH unit illuminated by the
sky light inside New Orleans
main airport, now the main
field hospital for victims
of Katrina. A week ago in
the airport, its long driveway
was lined with gas lanterns
to evoke the French Quarter.

This space, where travelers
had a cold beer before departure,
the ticket counters, luggage
belts still there but transformed
by their new desperate purpose.

A bar is now a make shift
pharmacy, the liquor bottles
replaced by tall stacks of
Tylenol, Ensure, Aciphlex
and alcohol preps, all under
a glowing Miller Light neon sign

New Orleans Airport Turned Field Hospital

the smell, sour and fetid.
Flies circled trash cans,
litter in corners. Bio hazards
with soiled diapers, soiled
clothes dirty gauze,
disposable gloves. Tents
where patients were being
treated were settled around
the terminal near the ticket
counter. Each had a sign
on the door. Red for
critical, yellow for semi
acute, green for primary
care. A doctor who just came
scribbled this on the inside
of her arm to remember

NEW ORLEANS AIRPORT HOSPITAL

Inside one tent, the
patients were lined up
on the floor. Many
came on stretchers
loaded with their
belongings—bags of
clothes, a pocket
book, a hat a wig,
a bible. One woman
brought her bird and
it chirped in its cage
beside her stretcher

SOME WERE MOANING, OTHERS SEEMED TO BE LOST IN A VACANT STATE OF RESIGNATION

one mother sat beside
her son, a 34 year old
paraplegic who had
been carried up eight
flights of darkened
stairs and evacuated
to the airport. Inside
the medic tent she
stroked her son's fore
head. His arms were
curled to his chest. His
mother took a towel
from her bag of
belongings and put
it on his arms so he
wouldn't get cold. "I am
not letting him out of
my sight" she said

As Many of the Refugees were Moved from Filthy

overheated, crime ridden
places like the Louisiana
Super Dome to decent
shelters, the value of each
item changed. Furs or
diamonds didn't matter.
But a clean pillow and
blanket. Or even a sheet,
could buy you anything:
diabetes meds, a piece of
meat. Office chairs with
wheels to ferry around
the ill and weak were worth
more than DVD players
and lap tops. Cigarettes
and liquor were initially
commodities, a comfort
in miserable conditions.
But the looters flooded the
market, there was so much
of the stuff people began
giving it away

Items Carried Out Take on New Weight

the waters raced into one
woman's home so quickly
she was forced to flee with
nothing but what she was
wearing. After she and ten
members of her extended
family took refuge in the
convention center down
town, she was grateful to
be on dry land but quickly
realized they had another
problem: aid workers
were giving out water and
food but there wasn't any
thing for her infant niece.
The only thing she had
that she thought might be
of value was the silver
necklace she was wearing

so she wandered around
the convention center for
hours trying to trade it
for milk. There were
no takers

ANOTHER WOMAN SAT IN A CHAIR PATIENTLY

she wore the same clothes
she had worn since she
and her husband were
evacuated. Wherever he
was going she was going.
"We've been married
50 years," she said,
holding her bible. "He's
never been on any airplane.
He needs me." But some
how in the confusion,
her husband was prepared
for transport, lifted, taken
off to a chopper and a
hospital. "He'll be scared
without me," she said,
clutching a bag of Cheezits
and her bible

AUTHOR BIOGRAPHY

Lyn Lifshin grew up in Barre and Middlebury Vermont and studied at Syracuse University, University of Vermont, Brandeis University and State University of New York at Albany. Lyn has written many books and edited 4 anthologies of women writers. Her poems have appeared in most poetry and literary magazines in the U.S.A, and her work has been included in virtually every major anthology of recent writing by women. She has given more than 700 readings across the U.S.A. and has appeared at Dartmouth and Skidmore Colleges, Cornell University, the Shakespeare Library, Whitney Museum, and Huntington Library.

Lyn has taught poetry and prose writing for many years at universities, colleges and high schools, and has been Poet in Residence at the University of Rochester, Antioch, and Colorado Mountain College. Winner of numerous awards including the Jack Kerouac Award for her book *Kiss The Skin Off*, Lyn is the subject of the documentary film *Lyn Lifshin: Not Made of Glass*. For her absolute dedication to the small presses which first published her, and for managing to survive on her own apart from any major publishing house or academic institution, Lyn Lifshin has earned the distinction, "Queen of the Small Presses." She has been praised by Robert Frost, Ken Kesey and Richard Eberhart. Ed Sanders has seen her as "a modern Emily Dickinson."

Her poem "No More Apologizing" has been called "among the most impressive documents of the women's poetry movement" by Alicia Ostriker. An update to her Gale Research Projects Autobiographical Series, "On the Outside, Lips, Blues, Blue Lace," was published in Spring, 2003.

Lyn spends her time between upstate New York and Nutley Pond, a goose pond in Virginia. She loves film, Abyssinian cats, dance and having all the snow go.

For interviews, more bio material, photographs, reviews, see her website: www.lynlifshin.com.

Breinigsville, PA USA
15 November 2010
249325BV00001B/8/P